Gautama Buddha
The Open Door of the Heart

THE TEMPLE OF THE PRESENCE®
The Ascended Master Wisdom delivered by
Monroe Julius Shearer & Carolyn Louise Shearer

Gautama Buddha:
The Open Door of the Heart

Published by
Acropolis Sophia Books & Works®
an imprint of
The Temple of The Presence®
P.O. Box 17839, Tucson, Arizona 85731

www.TempleofThePresence.org

Copyright © 1998, 1999, 2003, 2019, 2021 The Temple of The Presence, Inc.
All rights reserved.
No part of this book may be reproduced
in any form or by any means whatsoever without prior
written permission, except in the case of brief quotations
embodied in articles and reviews.

Cover Art Copyright © 2021 by The Temple of The Presence, Inc.

For information, write
Acropolis Sophia Books & Works®
P.O. Box 17839, Tucson, Arizona 85731

Printed in the United States of America
First Printing, 2021
Library of Congress Control Number: 2020952789
ISBN: 978-1-7337302-5-9

Dictations presented in *The Golden Gifts Series*
have been prepared by the presiding Master for
release in written form for our present use and
for posterity.

Table of Contents

Letter from the Anointed Representatives® 2

Expanding Your Detail Consciousness 5

*Know Your Heart and Anchor Its Light
   in the Earth* 13

The Pathway of the Heart 23

Keep the Flame Burning Brightly 33

Dear Students of the Ascended Masters and Disciples on the Path to Enlightenment,

It has long been our desire to share these Releases with you. Since the very beginning of The Temple of The Presence, Gautama Buddha has worked closely with the students of the Ascended Masters, teaching the Way of the Buddha and the Christ Consciousness. Throughout the ages, his Teaching and Instruction have led many disciples by the hand into his Flame of Peace, Compassion, Wisdom, and Love. And it is our fond hope that you, too, will discover his Flame and abide therein for a time, to learn at the feet of this Great Master.

The Dictations we share within this book have been carefully chosen and prepared so that you might enter into his Consciousness and Instruction effortlessly. In the Purity of the Truth of Cosmic Law®, his message has been given plainly and forthrightly so that you can know with absolute clarity the Wisdom of the Ages that will guide you along the Path that leads, not only to True Enlightenment, but to your Ascension in the Light.

As you pore over the words on these pages, the Buddha's tangible Presence can abide with you, even as it did during the original release of these Dictations. As you put your undivided attention upon his Flame, it can be as though you are present physically in the Sanctuary at Morya House, or in his Retreat at Shamballa, meditating in his Radiance and receiving his Teaching in real time. For his Presence is ever available for you to enter into.

The world knows Gautama Buddha as a great Teacher on the Path to Enlightenment. This we affirm as well, but we also know him to be an August Cosmic Being from the Secret Love Star who holds the Office of the Lord of the World. In this Office, with infinite Compassion and Love, he sustains the Heart Flames of the many Sons and Daughters of God across the face of the Earth. With the focus of his Consciousness, he breathes upon these most precious Sparks of the Threefold Flame so that mankind might continue to have the opportunity to expand that Flame and learn to walk the pathway to a Golden Age of One.

We invite you to take the time to study, read, and meditate upon these most precious Words from the Buddha. As you enter into your own Heart Flame of the Love, Wisdom, and Power of God, you likewise therein touch his Infinite Heart.

Come, enter into the Flame, and be at Peace.

Monroe Julius Shearer & *Carolyn Louise Shearer*

ANOINTED REPRESENTATIVES®
The Temple of The Presence®

Expanding Your Detail Consciousness

Allow Peace to flow through each cell. Allow Love to move out from your Heart. Allow Light to carry you up. Be Light and know the All-in-All. When you are in the Buddhic Light — the ALL, the Complete, the Whole of every Being — you want for nothing, for the Allness of The One is present where you are. Strive to attain the great Peace and Silence found only within the ALL.

As the noises of the world are buffeted away by the drops of rain[*], you will feel the sense of security and safety within the very sound of the raindrops. Allow your bodies to relax completely. Allow your mind to rest its weary, incessant, cognizing of thought. Then it is time for your Heart to move into action, for in the Silence your Heart is at home and able to conduct its own affairs.

---

[*] As this Dictation was being delivered, a gentle rain was falling. The raindrops hitting the metal roof of the building could be heard clearly during the Dictation.

As the Heart expands to become One with the ALL of the Silence, the Threefold Flame begins to burn more brightly. Then you can touch each Flame and understand, with greater sensitivity, the action of each Plume.

Attention to Detail

As God Love becomes the foundation for all of your life, you will discover that there is a greater impetus in your world for attending to even the minutest of details. You will find new meaning in those things that heretofore have been bothersome and agitating, and often totally neglected. For this expanded consciousness creates an enhanced awareness of detail. Receiving this detail consciousness, you become more keenly aware, not only of your own needs, but of the needs of others, and of just why Necessity demands accomplishment of certain given tasks.

Without this expanded awareness, many critical activities of the day would fall by the wayside without even one erg of your focused attention. This would be all well and good if all of those small details had no consequence. But you know not how gravely important many of those smallest details are to those momentous decisions you make or to your greater awareness of the Flame.

Begin and End Your Day in Your God Presence

There are no unimportant activities in your day. When arising in the morning, your first thought should be of your God Presence. When retiring at night, your last thought should be of your God Presence. Then all that transpires in between — all your comings and goings — will carry an increment of the Light of your God Presence registered upon them, for you will have established the right beginning and the right ending for your day.

Together with this expanded awareness, you will discover that by starting your day and ending your day correctly, the Flame of Love, the Flame of Illumination, and the Flame of the Will of God will weave a Pattern of Light within your Heart that touches all of those smaller activities and breathes Life into every aspect of your day, bringing greater meaning to everyone and everything that surrounds you.

The Heart Flame Will Focus Your Attention

You will find that the more you pay attention to the Flame on the Altar of your Heart, the more your attention will be galvanized to those details that are absolutely essential for you to focus on. This all sounds very simplistic, very easy, almost to a point of unimportance. But I wish to tell you that if you are to expand all of the Flames in all the chakras, learning how to use them, learning how not to misuse them, learning when to use them and when not to use them; if you are to allow for the Light of the Kundalini Fires to reach the height and the expanded growth throughout all of your chakras and all of the highways and byways that it will forge through; if there is to be God Vision and God Wisdom, then you must be able to take all of your surroundings, all of the energy and the subtlety in your life and bring them under the conscious control of the Mind of Christ. This exercise enables you to attain greater and greater adeptship in the use of the Light.

If you are accustomed to overlooking the supposedly small, unimportant details, if you have grown accustomed to having chaos, confusion, and disarray in your life, how will you ever be able to perceive the subtle flow of Light that must be extended from one or more chakras at a given time? For, you see, these spiritual actions are ofttimes far more subtle than handling the countless little details of your mundane life. You must be able to direct certain actions of the flow of Light into different areas or departments, if you will — thereby compartmentalizing not only the action, but the ability to wield the Light with a given direction and focus.

There are those advanced disciples who become so masterful that they can handle many things at one time, for they have this keen sense of awareness of all of the details. If you do not have this gift, then it is incumbent upon you to learn to focus your mind in a forward fashion on one thing at a time, making sure that the fullness of your attention is firmly fixed on that particular activity. If your mind has a tendency to be scattered or to waiver, you will not obtain the desired result, and your experiment will fail.

First you learn to handle one minute detail with ease, then add a second simultaneously, and then another upon accomplishing that one, and another until, before you know it, you have acquired the ability to apportion the energy that you are working with and deal decisively with a multitude of different areas, different levels, and even different awarenesses within your own consciousness simultaneously.

Become Master of All the Rays

Many of the actions that you will become adept in using will only be applicable to specific aspects of the Law. In other situations, you will find other chakras and other Rays much more beneficial, so you should not spend all of your time and energy focused on only one action of the Law. It is necessary for you to expand your knowledge and awareness of all of the Seven Rays for you to know when one given Ray's operation is not the most effective, requiring another to be used in its place. I realize this all sounds hypothetical, but I assure you it is grounded in very specific actions of the Law.

Allow your Heart to weave the Light that will touch each action required in your day. Begin and end your day in the Heart of the Silence as you place your attention upon your own God Presence, and all the actions of the Law will come about in their correct order, nurtured by the Flame on the Altar of your Heart.

There are Ascended Masters who can teach you to structure and prioritize all your activities. Beloved Leto is one. She can help you organize your day if you will call to Her. But if you find that you have difficulty expanding the Flame on your Heart to enter into the Joy of attending to the small details of your life, you may call to Me. For I, Gautama, do place my attention upon every small detail, upon every one of the many millions of Heart Flames that are entrusted to my keeping.

I Hold You in the Flame of My Heart

The focus of my awareness for you is to hold you in the Flame of my Heart. Every day I touch the Heart of each unascended lifestream with a very specific release from my own Heart.

For I, the Buddha, sit in contemplation upon God, not only at the beginning and the end of cycles, but throughout Eternity.

Know that you are in my Heart and I AM in yours and be at Peace with the Joy of your newfound appreciation for attention to detail.

As you hear each drop of rain, trace that drop with the fingers of your mind, with the petals of your Heart, and with the rhythm of the Mighty Inbreath and the Outbreath of Cosmic Cycles. When you can touch each drop of rain, you will be where I AM.

Gautama

Know Your Heart and Anchor its Light in the Earth

Beloved Ones,
There are those who have yet to experience the Heart — the Essence of the Fullness of Life, of your Life. If you are to understand the God Life of an Ascended Master, you must start by discovering your own Heart.

There are those who do not know or understand the feeling that flows from your Heart — the Fire, the Vibration, and the Signal that you send to one another and to all of life. Your Heart, beloved ones, emanates Light twenty-four hours a day from beginning to end and for beginnings without end throughout a lifetime. And when the physical body is no more, your Heart returns to Higher Octaves to be protected, nourished, and safeguarded until your next opportunity to embody.

Your Heart is a Flame that is Never Extinguished

Your Heart, beloved ones, is a Flame, a Flame that never burns out, as it is constantly nourished by the Mighty I AM Presence and by my Heart. For I, Gautama, hold your Heart in my Hand, extending the very Essence of my Flame to you. To receive the full benefit of my Grace requires that you place your attention, each and every day, in a very quiet manner, upon the Essence of your Being, your very own Heart.

Your Heart will speak to you in vibration. Many expect to hear an audible voice, but train your attention to become attentive to the subtleties and shifts of the vibrations that register directly upon the Heart. You will also discover through experience that there are times when it is necessary to speak through a more than ordinary pressure — through your Heart — of a particular God Quality such as Love, Patience, Wisdom, Understanding, and, as Morya says, Tolerance.

Place Your Attention Upon God

There are many who are very confused about this individual Path of the Ascension. I would like to explain. There need be no confusion. It is most simple. First you place your attention upon God. Then you become God in Action. And then you become One with all of Life. It is most easy to manifest — you place your attention upon God, and you become God in Action.

There are many who prefer to place their attention upon all of the trappings of the physical world. If you are unfamiliar with my teachings or my own life as Gautama, perhaps you should familiarize yourself with these teachings. For you will discover that, yes, as a young child I was shielded from the world. I knew not of sin, disease, and death. I knew only the inherited desires of the flesh. They are not much different from sin, disease, and death — for all are desires, whether they be for pleasure or for pain, beloved ones — desires that take your attention away from your Oneness with your own God Presence.

This does not mean that you cannot have the Fullness of the true Joys and the Beauty that Life affords you. This does not mean that you cannot express the right action that you are to manifest through your work or through your communications. Hear what I AM saying. You must place your attention upon God. God is in all of Life. God is in the Beauty, in the music, in the art, in the good works. It is all a matter of your perception.

When you choose to align your perception and the energies of your being with negativity, with that which is ungodly and uncomfortable and assails the Purity of your Heart, you will discover a sense of anxiety in your world and feel separation from that Heart. For some, only a small correction will be necessary to realign yourself. For others, a complete shift of consciousness, of habit, and of desire will be required.

Those who think that worldly desires and endeavors offer the fullness of living have never tasted the Waters, the Living Waters of the Light of their own God Presence. They have not yet touched the hem of the Garment of an Ascended

Being or felt the reverberation in their world of the emanation of the Essence of that Ascended One. You must witness to them so they understand that there is so much more to life.

Use Discernment in Witnessing

But before doing so, await the invitation from their lifestream. It is a zen action of the Law. You must be the one to discern if that one has reached out and sent the signal from their Heart or their lips that they desire to know more. For you see, beloved ones, if understanding of the Truth of Life is not desired, it cannot become a part of any lifestream. Not unlike yourself, for you cannot become anything that you do not first desire. The choices are always yours. They are made daily.

The Ascended Masters would guide you to the Higher Vibrations and the Higher Octaves of Light. They alone know that you must first lower your own Wedding Garment into your world from those Higher Octaves before fulfilling all that you really desire to become at the core level of your being.

It is not enough to simply say you want your Ascension. Even though Ascended Master students hold the goal of the Ascension foremost in their consciousness, the goal is not to escape. It is not to move away from the Earth. It is to draw into the Earth every Vibration of God Reality.

Ascensions Bring Greater Light to the Earth

As more and more internalize the Fire of their own God Presence and expand the Light upon their Heart, you will discover a new world, a new vibration in which to live and move. You will discover that you have more ease in communicating with your associates and having them in your presence. There will be more comfort, for lo and behold, as there are more Ascensions and more expansion of the Light upon the Heart, there will be a Higher Vibration radiating throughout the Earth. For when one Son or Daughter of God reaches high and allows for the Octaves of Light to be anchored into the Earth, all in the Earth are the beneficiaries — each and every lifestream, as well as all of elemental life and all substance. But there must first be the pure desire for God.

I, the Buddha, continue to place my attention upon God and hold it fast. I have done so since my Enlightenment. I AM aware of the Heart Flames I touch, but my Consciousness is so tethered to the Buddhic Level of Consciousness in the Octaves of Light that the Rays going forth from my Heart contact only the Pure Essence of your own Heart. For no vibration less than the God Vibration can be present as my Light moves through all worlds.

The Path of the Integration of the Light

Anchoring this Light into the Earth is what you have taken embodiment to master. This is the Path, and it is entirely within your grasp! Every day there arise new opportunities to integrate the Light of God into your life. Yes, I and Morya sing the same song, for the desire for the Will of God is the most important aspect in both of our lives and burns brightly in our desire for God.

Do not shun this opportunity. Do not think that you have passed your prime — the time in your life when you could still accomplish all that you came to do. Do not consider that you are too young and that there are other things you should be placing your attention upon. For I promise that if you place the full weight of your desire upon God, God will not let you down, and you will receive the greatest reward.

That reward may not reflect the color, the density, or the substance that you anticipated, for in many cases the Reality of God is much simpler, purer, and quieter than you ever thought possible. Why even this moment is a test for some to sit still. This should tell you how impatient and unruly the outer bodies have become. So it is important to learn to discipline those outer bodies that they not overrule your True Being. Let your Heart take command of all of your vehicles and then observe as they perform their Perfect Work.

Become acquainted with your Heart. Allow your Heart to act in your life. Know that your Heart will never fail you, because the Flame upon the Altar of that Heart is the Heart of your own God Presence.

I, Gautama, seal your Heart with the Fullness of the Love of my Heart for God, that you might dwell within this Protective Envelope while you are learning to trust your very own Heart and become more and more of God until that God Life overflows into every facet of your life.

AUM — AUM — AUM

Gautama

The Pathway of the Heart

Blessed Children,
I AM here. And I entreat you into the Heart of the Buddha, a Heart which truly knows Compassion and which desires to share this wealth of understanding of the true Compassion to all of life.

Many desire to love. But when love has attachment, it cannot flow freely. It is held in bondage, sadly never touching the object of its desiring. Know well that when a Heart has been stirred by the Vibration of Pure Love, other Hearts may respond in their purest nature. When your foremost desire is to be loved, that which you send forth returns in like manner. Put away all preoccupation with what you thought to be the nature of love. Enter instead into the Heart of the Fullness of the Wealth of God Love.

Hold Fast to Your Divine Image

As you perceive life, you impose upon life the concept of your own subjective perceptions. You paint the portrait of your very own image, first desiring this look and then that, not taking into consideration that at the Core of your Being resides the Image of the I AM. This Image, ever so Perfect, the Radiance of Holiness and the Vibration of Love fashioned by the Hand of God, is who you, beloved, should be desiring to be.

Hold fast to this Perfect Image. Hold it as the Single-Eyed Vision in your mind. Trace and retrace with the fingers of emotion the movement, the Scintillating Vibration that brings together every cell, every atom into the perfected form of your Vision. As you allow the Heart of Compassion to bring into the fullness of your desiring that which is God, that which is Perfect, that which is Holy, your Image will surely come to pass. For it is the desiring of the Heart, the fashioning of the mind, and the energy-in-motion that allows you to bring forth all manner of creation. But, most especially, it is the Image that you project upon the screen of the physical plane as your Identity.

Oh, for years you have considered you were fashioned by your earthly parents. But know, beloved, that at a point in your life your own Christed Identity will step forth and bring into perfect view, for all to see, the Radiance of the Light emanating from a Heart that knows itself as the Heart of the I AM, that has within it the Perfect Blueprint, not only of that which you are to present to life, but that which you are to accomplish, to master, and to establish as Attainment and Virtue of your own making.

Each Footstep is Important

That which you perceive within the mind and send forth as the desiring of your Heart, as Compassion and Love, that, too, is your own, beloved. It is the creation of your making at the election of the I AM. As you traverse the Earth, numbered among all the Sons and Daughters of God, your footsteps are counted, determined, steadfast, ever-constant, determining the right course and, at the election of the Mind of God, choosing those areas of life in which to become invested.

Perhaps you did not consider how very important are your footsteps in determining the course of your Path. Consider that when your feet are anchored within the Rod of Power, as the integration of your vehicles of consciousness, and you are firmly planted within the Mission and the Divine Plan of your lifestream, the very steps that you take are guided by the Mind of God, are moved by the Love bringing forth the desiring of the Compassionate Heart. Most assuredly, the energy-in-motion within you facilitates the pace with which you stride forward. Is it constant and steadfast or irregular and jagged?

The Figure-Eight Flow

The Christ knows only to move within the dictates of the Heart and by the determined action of the Mind of God. The resilience of the Power of God, as the integration of the Rod of Power, allows for the vertical figure-eight flow between the Heart of the initiate and the Heart of God.

This figure-eight flow develops momentum, accelerating with the Constancy of the determination of your Heart, and with this acceleration the stepped-up vibration of all that is endeavored by the Christ, allowing for each step to be a calculated, perfect, and absolute right direction, right action, right accomplishment. For all of the integration of your Being has held fast within your Heart, bringing forth the Fullness of your Divine Plan as orchestrated by your own God Presence.

One Buddhic-Christic Heart and Path

Now you have said, "Why is the Buddha speaking of the Christ? Is not the Path of the Buddha unique unto itself, a discipline, a course of action, and a way of life that is separate and apart from the Way of the Christ?" At first blush, those unschooled in the intricacies of the Heart of the Buddha and the Heart of the Christ might consider that these Paths are different indeed. But when you strip away human perception, human labels, and the layers of maya and illusion that are wont to gravitate around any discipline, you will find at the very core of the Heart of the Buddha and the Heart of the Christ one and the same Heart.

For each is fashioned of the Threefold Flame. Each is nourished by the Threefold Flame of the

I AM THAT I AM. Each steps forth to accomplish the Fullness of its Mission. Those fully understanding the Ways of the Buddha know that life is Mastery. Life is Virtue. Life is bringing forth Perfection and True Vibration into all its avenues. Life is to be lived in the Fullness of the Vibration of the I AM. Life is to discover Mastery and Victory in every area of accomplishment, leading to the ultimate Oneness with God, the I AM THAT I AM.

Therefore, the Way of the Buddha is the Path of Christhood. It consists of the Christic Virtues held fast by the Teachings of Maitreya, by the guiding hand of Krishna, and by the full integration of every Buddha who ever walked the Earth. Each one who steps forth in the Fullness of the Christ Virtues is likewise exhibiting the Fullness of the Path of the Buddha, for the Eightfold Path is a part of the whole of the Virtues of the Christ. The Fullness of the Refuge in the Buddha is the wearing of the Garment of Christhood. The understanding of the Laws of God as they are inherent within the Earth is the greater Teaching of the Christ.

As you place your attention upon your own Threefold Flame, you will find that you have also entered into the Heart of the Buddha. You will weave the Garment of the Christ. And you will understand the integration of Wholeness on the Path of Mastery and Attainment to the Ascension.

You Have Been Prepared

In past eras, it was not possible to reach the consciousness of certain lifestreams predisposed to a particular religious dogma. They would have found the Teachings that you study today impossible to adopt, for they had not been prepared. You, however, have been through many incarnations in the Earth. You have studied in the Retreats of the Ascended Masters. You have absorbed into your conscious awareness a greater understanding of the inclusive Path that holds within it the Cosmic Law as set forth by the God of Very Gods, continually revealed to enable mankind's awareness to expand in attainment.

The expansion continues first within one individual and then another and another until it encompasses the community, the country, and the world. This allows for a new level of Teaching and Understanding to be brought forth and for there to be a stripping away of all superstition, which is wont to find its way into every teaching after a time. Guard against superstition. When the Heart is firmly fixed to vibrate to its fullest throughout all of the affairs of your life, you will not be inclined to rest upon old superstitions that would keep you locked into a matrix that does not allow you to expand or to receive new instruction. This, beloved, has been the stalemate of many generations. Only after a number of incarnations have those superstitions been eroded by the passing of karmic ties and a greater opportunity of awakening to more of the reality of the Heart.

The Perfect Path of Initiation

The Heart is where we began and where we will always end. For through each incarnation you traverse worlds via the pathway of the Heart. Those who make the greatest acceleration in their own attainment are those who embrace the Heart steadfastly and confidently, allowing the Compassion of the Heart to flow and the Mind of God to be in action with their Heart. Their feet are anchored by the Rod of Power which is the integration of the Christic Virtues with the outer vehicles of consciousness of their individual lifestream.

This would seem to be a Perfect Path and a Perfect Teaching, would it not? But do not get too comfortable, for when you do, your own Holy Christ Presence will begin to open up new avenues, new awareness, and new opportunities to engage the Heart. That is the way of all Life. That is the Path of the Buddha and the Christ. This is the Path of Initiation.

The Path will always remain Perfect so long as you hold to the Perfect Vibration of Ascended Master Consciousness. Hold fast to your expanding awareness, that it abides in the Vibration of the Heart of God, for it is there you will know the Pure Path of the Bodhisattvas and the Buddhas who have gone before. You will understand the Teachings of the Christ and of the Christic Line that have moved through the Initiatic Path of the Christ, and you will be able to embrace the wider circle of opportunity that is afforded the Christ and the Buddha as One.

It is my Joy to release my Radiation into the Earth during this perfect time when the riptides of negative emotions are not reacting upon the precious chakras of the children of God. It is my desire for you to have the Radiance of the Sun-Behind-the-Sun directly infusing your Being — the Being of Light that you are, the Being of Joy, and the Being of Compassion you are becoming. Accept within every cell of your being, within every erg of energy, within every plane of consciousness, the Pure Light of the Sun and of the Heart of Gautama.

My Heart is with you. My Heart is devoted to you. My Heart is One with you.

 AUM.

   AUM.

     AUM.

Gautama

Keep the Flame Burning Brightly

Blessed Children of the Light,
You have entered into the Buddhic Consciousness of my Flame. Within this Consciousness you have clarity of mind. But most importantly, you have established the Abiding Peace that allows for you to experience the Unity of all that you are in The One. The thoughts that you might have, the beating of the physical heart, the emotions swirling round about, all are caught up into the swirling action of the Threefold Flame of the Heart, elevating you into the lofty state of awareness that the outer form is nothing compared to the Higher Form and Light of the Presence of God.

So much attention is given to the outer vehicles, it is a wonder that anyone ever knows of the Presence.

And yet, the Flame upon the Altar of your Heart has reminded you, has captured your attention, and ultimately filled your outer chalice so that you have become aware. You have separated yourself out from the mass consciousness and adopted the Truth of your God Identity.

When I come and speak directly to that Heart Flame, you must be aware that there is a surge of my Light that occurs, a Scintillating Fire that begins an active, swirling action that lifts your spirits, allows for the burdens of everyday life to be lifted off your shoulders, penetrates your consciousness to bring stillness so that the outer mind is not flitting to and fro, and you have the ability to allow the saturation of the Buddhic Realm to enter into your mind as the Presence of your Christ Mind.

The Peace that is established within your emotions begins to take on greater importance. For you become aware that that is the power center of your being. For when you have not depleted your emotions and they are held in check, you can engage on the instant with the Mind of God, the flow of the Love of God, and the Purity that surrounds you. For indeed the very Presence of the Almighty would not send you forth into a wasteland, void of all of the Pristine Perfection eternally held in the Mind of God.

Surrounding you is the All-in-All of God, but what remains are your outer vehicles. Are you able to sense the Allness of God with your outer senses? Have they been trained to look beyond that which does not hold to the Pattern of Perfection, piercing through the veils of maya and illusion to see the Beauty of God? Have your vehicles been trained to feel the flow of the Current of the Presence, saturating the atmosphere about you, giving you Comfort and Love and the Harmony that brings forth wholeness, health, and wellbeing?

And then the physical body has the opportunity to truly move with those Currents in the rhythm and flow of the Light of the Mighty I AM Presence, giving it Strength and yes, Courage. Because absent the Courage to move forward, many times you are at a stalemate in life, not able to enter into the many Dispensations afforded you — opportunities and open doors that the Presence has worked mightily to prepare for you. So as this

Flame excites all that is good within you — to accelerate, to move forward in life — you begin to realize that God is Good and that Goodness is your Mighty I AM Presence.

I, Gautama, know well what many have said were the teachings of my era that supposedly were passed down by me. Many were passed down over generations by mere word of mouth, by what the consciousness of a devotee or a passerby could remember. But when those consciousnesses were commingled with the substance of unreality still pervasive within their minds, you can begin to see how I was many times misquoted. Consequently, the Pure Understanding of the Buddha was not held in the Fullness of the Charge of the Intent of the Brotherhood of Light.

You must hold fast, even now, to what you receive in the Purity of the Charge of Light so that you will not commingle Cosmic Law with your misperceptions of what you think the meaning is. Allow the Flame upon the Altar of your Heart to continue to illumine you and bring an understanding of the meaning that is passed to you. For you are the one out of the many who will have to pass on the Truth of Cosmic Law®, first and foremost, in the example of your life, then in what you do with that Teaching — how you convey it, how you live it.

The Fullness of the Light of your Mighty I AM Presence will always keep you in the Purity of the Truth of your Identity and how accurately you receive the Cosmic Law that you are given. But you must work mightily to hold onto it. Prepare your vehicles so that they do not spin out into the mass consciousness, absorbing into your mind and emotions distortions from those undetected influences of the mass consciousness.

O blessed hearts, there is much psychism in the world. Do not fall prey to it. For future generations depend upon you and what you will accomplish.

The Purity of the Flame of God shines ever brightly. That is the Light that we see round about you here and even in your own private sanctuary. For you invoke that Light, and it is that Light that serves the Flame upon the Altar of your Heart, that will teach, feed, and heal your vehicles of consciousness.

Let the Wholeness come forth and keep you all the days of your life so that when you are called to return Home, you will already be there in the Heart of your own Threefold Flame, overshadowed by your own Christ Consciousness and the streaming forth of the Buddhic Web of the Mind of God.

That is the Action which We, the Ascended Masters, hold in our Heart, our Consciousness, our Visualization for you so that you will not miss such a Glorious Opportunity that Life has extended to you by the Hand of God. All comes from God, you know: the very air that you breathe, the beating of your physical heart, the sounds you hear that are beautiful, harmonious, melodic.

When you allow your inner ear to attune to the Inner Spheres, you realize the Soundless Sound of the Angels, of the Currents of Light and Momentum. And then that Sound begins to mold and shape the patterns that you move in throughout your day, while occupying your physical body. Such is the integration with the Buddhic Realm that you are called to participate in — to live within! That is the manifest Glory of God!

Let the Fire of the Buddhic Web be ever in attendance to your conscious awareness, illumining your thoughts, conducting your affairs and your life, establishing patterns of Wholeness, and knitting together the creative genius of your own God Presence streaming forth. For is that not the desire of the heart of many — to bring forth to the best of their ability gifts that will benefit all, most especially the Presence of God?

Let the gifts of your life and the fulfillment of your Divine Plan be placed upon the High Altar of your own God Presence. Continue to nurture that Communion from the beginning of a creative idea all the way to the manifestation of that ideal momentum or creativity. Hold fast the *Thread of Contact* with all that you have ever placed upon the Altar of the Most High. This, blessed ones, is an important key to your ability to truly stay within the Current of Light of the Presence while you bring forth into manifestation, on all of the planes of God Consciousness, what your Mighty I AM still desires of you. Let all your desiring be the desires of the Presence!

Hold fast to the Heartbeat of God that blazes upon the Altar of your Heart! Let the Current of the swirling action carry you aloft into the Consciousness of your God Presence, allowing for the streaming Patterns of the Ideal Life that you can live. Yes, an Ideal, Perfect Life is what the Will of God intends for you. But you must understand that you must make it so and you must live it. That is the Glorious Gift that I, Gautama, have for you on this Celebration of Wesak: that you would know who you are and how special you are in the sight of God!

Let the Light that I stream forth keep you in this momentum of acceleration all the days of your life and beyond into the Ascension! For yes, blessed ones, I see you entering into the Blessed Union with the Mighty I AM Presence, and I patiently await that day, all the while you are about the Work that your Presence desires.

Keep the Flame burning brightly! For that, blessed ones, is your Life.

I, Gautama, commend you for reaching the Attainment that you have to consciously receive me. And I support you in your further acceleration in the Light.

Lord Gautama

We welcome you to become a
Torch Bearer of The Temple®
in a Sacred Covenant with
Beloved Saint Germain and
the Brotherhood's Mission through
The Temple of The Presence.®

If you would like more information on
becoming a Torch Bearer or on
The Temple of The Presence,
please call us at
520-751-2039
or visit our website at
www.templeofthepresence.org.

You are also invited to connect with us
on Facebook and Instagram.

We are so grateful you have heard the Words of the Ascended Masters and have recognized the Light of their Consciousness going forth into the world.